My Little Book of
Rocks, Minerals, and Gems

by Claudia Martin

Quarto is the authority on a wide range of topics.

Quarto educates, entertains and enriches the lives of our readers—enthusiasts and lovers of hands-on living.

www.quartoknows.com

Words in **bold** are explained in the glossary on page 60.

Publisher: Maxime Boucknooghe
Editorial Director: Victoria Garrard
Art Director: Miranda Snow
Design and editorial: Tall Tree Ltd

First published in the United States by QEB Publishing
Part of The Quarto Group
6 Orchard, Lake Forest, CA 92630

A CIP record for this book is available from the Library of Congress

ISBN 978 1 68297 147 5

Manufactured in Guangdong, China TT092017
9 8 7 6 5 4 3 2

Contents

Our rocky planet

4   What is rock?
6   What is a mineral?
8   How rocks are formed
10   Changing rocks
12   Humans and rocks
14   Fossils

Igneous rocks

16   Igneous rock spotter
18   Basalt
20   Obsidian
22   Pumice

Metamorphic rocks

24   Metamorphic rock spotter
26   Marble
28   Slate

Sedimentary rocks

30   Sedimentary rock spotter
32   Chalk
34   Clay
36   Coal
38   Limestone

Minerals

40   Mineral spotter
42   Metals
44   Silicates
46   Carbonates
48   Minerals all around us
50   Minerals for industry

Gems

52   Gem spotter
54   Diamond
56   Silicon gems
58   Ruby and sapphire

60   Glossary
62   Index

What is rock?

The Earth is covered in a thick layer of **rock**. Rock lies beneath the oceans and underneath the soil in which plants grow.

« Some rocks are soft and crumbly. This is chalk.

« Many rocks are hard enough to build with. St Paul's Cathedral in London, UK, is made from limestone.

The Earth's outer layer of **solid** rock is called its **crust**. There are hundreds of different types of rocks in the crust. They have many colors, patterns, and uses.

⌄ These rocks in California aren't covered in soil, so we can take a good look at them.

What is a mineral?

All rocks are mixtures of different **minerals**. Minerals are solids. They are formed in the ground or in water.

˅ **The mineral quartz is made of the elements silicon and oxygen.**

« **Granite is a hard rock made out of the minerals quartz, feldspar, and mica.**

Minerals are made of **elements**. Elements are the building blocks for everything on Earth. The most common elements in the Earth's crust are silicon and oxygen.

The elements in a mineral are linked in a pattern. If a mineral has room to grow, it keeps on building the same pattern—making a regular shape called a **crystal**.

⌃ These crystals of aragonite have formed a cluster.

How rocks are formed

There are three groups of rocks.
Each group is formed in a different way.

Sedimentary rock is made when bits of rocks, minerals, or plants are pressed together for thousands of years.

<< **Sedimentary rock layers can sometimes be seen in cliff faces.**

Beneath the Earth's crust is hot, melted rock called **magma**. When magma cools, it becomes **igneous** rock. Igneous rock is the most common type of rock.

Deep underground, rocks come under great heat and **pressure**. This changes them into a new type of rock—**metamorphic** rock.

⌄ **Serpentine is used in buildings. It is a metamorphic rock.**

⌃ **Sometimes hot liquid rock bursts out of a volcano.**

Changing rocks

Our rocks are slowly changing. Some are being worn away by wind and rain. Others are being pushed to the Earth's surface.

∧ Sand is bits of broken rock. If sand is buried and pressed for a very long time, it will turn into sandstone.

On the Earth's surface, rocks are battered by frost, wind, rain, and rivers. Over many years, they are worn away or broken into pieces. These pieces may become new sedimentary, igneous, or metamorphic rocks.

>> If sandstone gets very, very hot, it becomes quartzite.

<< This sandstone arch in Utah was carved by the wind and rain. Sandstone is a sedimentary rock.

11

Humans and rocks

Humans have always found lots of uses for rocks and minerals.

<< These stone ax heads were made 5000 years ago in the Swiss Alps.

More than 3 million years ago, our ancestors were using rocks as tools and weapons. Today, we use rocks and minerals to make buildings, jewelry, and roads.

>> Some minerals are valued for their clearness, hardness, or color. They are called gems.

∨ This machine is digging rock from a quarry to use in buildings.

13

Fossils

When an animal or plant dies, it can leave a mark or its remains in a rock or mineral. This is a **fossil**.

>> This dinosaur died 150 million years ago. Its bones have been preserved in rock.

⌄ This bug got stuck in tree resin. Over millions of years the resin hardened into amber.

Fossils are often found in sedimentary rocks. Over millions of years, the remains of a plant or animal have been pressed under sand or mud until they harden.

⌄ **This dinosaur footprint was left in mud 200 million years ago. The mud hardened into rock.**

Igneous rock spotter

There are over 700 types of igneous rocks. Here are some tips for telling them apart.

⌄ **Pegmatite is formed when magma cools very slowly. Its crystals are big.**

Igneous rocks are made of different sorts of cooled magma. When it cools slowly, the minerals grow into large crystals. If it cools fast, the crystals stay small.

<< Rhyolite is formed when magma is thrown from a volcano and cools quickly. Its crystals are very small.

<< Granite is formed below ground from cooled magma. It is pushed above ground by movements in the crust.

Basalt

Basalt forms when runny magma pours out of a volcano, or bubbles up onto the seabed, and cools quickly.

« Basalt is gray, but it often turns reddish. This is because its minerals contain iron, which rusts.

Basalt contains the minerals feldspar, pyroxene, and olivine. Its crystals are small. As basalt cools, it sometimes cracks into strange columns.

⌄ **The Giant's Causeway in Northern Ireland is a famous basalt formation.**

>> **Here, basalt has cooled underwater, making curious pillow shapes.**

Obsidian

Obsidian is a hard, dark-colored igneous rock. It is made when magma erupts from a volcano and cools down fast.

Obsidian cools so quickly that its minerals do not have time to grow crystals at all. This makes it shiny, hard, and very sharp when broken.

>> Obsidian rocks lie everywhere on Glass Mountain, an ancient volcano in California.

>> Ancient peoples made blades from obsidian. This razor-sharp knife was used by the Aztecs of Central America.

Pumice

Pumice is full of holes. It is formed when super-hot and gassy magma is hurled out of a volcano.

<< Pumice is rough. It is used to rub away dead skin on your feet.

As bubbles of **gas** escape from the magma, it becomes frothy. The same thing happens when you open a bottle of soda!

23

Metamorphic rock spotter

Metamorphic rocks are made when any sort of rock is changed by great heat and pressure. Here's how to spot them.

Movements in the Earth's crust can create so much pressure that rock will bend and fold. A great way to spot metamorphic rocks is to look for stripes, folds, or layers.

>> Schist formed when rocks such as mudstone were pressed and folded deep underground.

<< Hornfels was baked by the heat given off by magma. This chunk is striped.

∧ You may often find gneiss on mountains where rocks have been pushed upward. It has dark and light bands.

Marble

Marble is limestone that has been heated. It can be beautifully colored, from pink and blue to green and black.

>> Marble is often used in buildings. The Taj Mahal in India is made from marble.

⌃ This marble is a deep purple color and richly patterned.

Limestone is usually pale, giving pure marble a white color. Sometimes miniclay, sand, or iron minerals are in the limestone. When the limestone is pressed and heated, these minerals create swirling colored patterns.

Slate

Slate is formed when shale is pressed by movements in the Earth's crust. Shale is a sedimentary rock made of mud and clay.

<< **This modern house has been built with slate bricks.**

The crystals in slate are pushed into layers. These layers are easy to split into flat sheets. The sheets are useful for roof and floor tiles.

∨ You can sometimes find fossils in slate. This sea animal was buried in mud and clay 500 million years ago.

« For thousands of years, people have dug slate from quarries.

Sedimentary rock spotter

It is quite easy to spot sedimentary rocks, because they are common on the Earth's surface. Here are clues to look for.

« Conglomerate rock consists of separate pebbles and small rocks stuck together by hardened clay and sand.

Sedimentary rocks are made when pebbles, sand, mud, plants, or minerals are pressed together. This makes them softer and crumblier than other rocks. You may see layers or grains of different materials.

<< The layers of sandstone rock are easy to spot in the Grand Canyon. The newest layers are at the top.

Chalk

Chalk is formed when tiny shells fall to the seafloor. Over thousands of years, the shells are crushed until they harden.

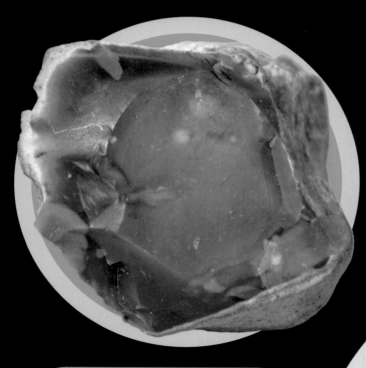

Chalk is worn away by waves, wind, and rain more slowly than other rocks. As a result, we can often see chalk cliffs at the seaside, and chalk hills in the countryside.

⌃ Lumps of flint can be found in chalk. Flint is made when the mineral quartz grows among the seashells.

» The White Cliffs of Dover, UK, are the world's most famous chalk cliffs. They rise to 360 feet high.

» Chalk cliffs and hills are a great place to spot the fossils of ancient sea creatures.

Clay

Clay is a very soft sedimentary rock. It forms when minerals and plants collect at the bottom of lakes and oceans.

>> These beautiful clay cliffs are in Massachusetts.

<< Clay is perfect for making pots. The minerals kaolinite and illite give clay a brown or orangey color.

Clay contains a lot of water. When clay is wet, it is easy to shape. When clay is heated, it hardens. This makes clay very useful for creating plates, bowls, and sculptures.

>> In China, the Terracotta Army was made out of clay more than 2200 years ago.

Coal

Coal is a sedimentary rock. It is made of rotted plants, which fell to the ground millions of years ago.

⌄ **These coal miners in Russia are using a drill to mine coal from a coal** seam.

After the plants fell, they were buried under layers of sand and mud. Over time, they formed a hard, black rock. Coal burns well, which makes it useful as a **fuel**.

>> A layer of coal is sandwiched between other rocks.

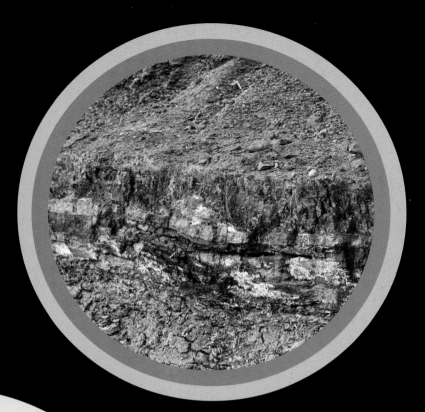

<< Coal is called a "fossil fuel" because it is made of dead plants that have been fossilized.

Limestone

Limestone is made of the shells and skeletons of shellfish and corals. It took millions of years to form.

⩔ **These famous tooth-shaped peaks are in Guilin, China. They were made when limestone was slowly washed away by water.**

Limestone dissolves easily in water. This means that it can mix with, and become part of, water. Where limestone is dissolved by rainwater or rivers, it can create strange shapes and caves.

⌃ Water has carved cracks in this limestone in Yorkshire, UK. Now it looks like paving stones.

« This limestone cave in Germany was made by an underground river.

Mineral spotter

There are over 4600 minerals. Good places to spot them are beaches, riverbeds, and—if you are careful—old quarries.

⌃ **Epidote forms tall, green-colored crystals.**

Most minerals form when elements join together. Different minerals contain different elements, such as silicon and oxygen, or calcium and carbon. When the elements join, they create crystals of different shapes and colors.

⌄ **Pyrite contains iron and sulfur. It is sometimes called "fool's gold."**

⌃ **These unusually perfect blue crystals are the mineral azurite.**

Metals

Metals such as gold, silver, and copper are actually minerals. Metals are hard and shiny.

« Pure silver is very hard to find. We use it for mirrors, jewelry, and electric devices.

Unlike most minerals, metal minerals contain just one element. Metals are very useful, which is why they have been mined for thousands of years.

⌄ **Copper often grows in branching clusters. It has a red-gold color.**

« **Gold nuggets can be found in rocks. Gold's bright color makes it popular for jewelry.**

43

Silicates

Silicates are minerals that have silicon and oxygen as their main ingredients. Most rocks contain silicate minerals.

The most common elements in the Earth's crust are silicon and oxygen. It is no surprise that silicate minerals are the most common minerals of all.

« Lazurite is given its beautiful blue color by the element sulfur.

⌄ Clear quartz crystals contain only silicon and oxygen. This quartz also contains iron, which makes it yellow.

⌄ Jadeite is a very rare mineral. Its green color comes from the elements chromium and iron.

Carbonates

The key ingredients in **carbonate** minerals are carbon and oxygen. Most carbonates are pale colored and soft.

⌄ **You might see calcite crystals around** hot springs **and in caves.**

⌃ **In caves, aragonite crystals can make flower shapes.**

Carbonate minerals usually form near water. They can be found on seabeds, around hot springs, and in damp caves. The minerals calcite and aragonite are also produced by sea creatures, to make their shells.

>> Limestone is made from shells, so it contains aragonite and calcite.

Minerals all around us

Did you know that minerals are all around us, in our kitchens, on our desks, and on our bathroom shelves?

« Fluorite crystals are broken down to get the element fluoride. It is put in toothpaste to make teeth strong.

If you look carefully, you can find minerals everywhere. The "lead" in your pencil is actually the mineral graphite. Inside your watch may be a tiny quartz crystal that makes it tick evenly.

Minerals for industry

From farming to making computers and blowing glass, every industry uses minerals.

Over 60 minerals are used to make every computer. Its metals, such as aluminum, copper, and gold, are taken from minerals. Calcite and other carbonates are used to make its plastic keyboard.

>> **Apatite contains the element phosphorus. It is used in** fertilizers, **which farmers spread on fields.**

⌃ Cinnabar contains the element mercury. Mercury is used in many electric devices.

⌃ Feldspar minerals help to make glass stronger.

Gem spotter

Only 130 minerals are considered to be gems, so you will be very lucky if you spot one in a rock!

Gems are minerals that are so sparkling or colorful that people want to wear them as jewelry. Most gems are very hard, because no one wants to pay for a jewel that could smash.

« Opal is popular because of its shimmering rainbow of colors.

>> Many gems are prized for their clearness. These gems are different colors of tourmaline.

>> Grandidierite is one of the rarest and most expensive gems.

Diamond

Diamond is a mineral containing only one element: carbon. It is the hardest mineral of all.

⌄ Before it is cut and polished, a "rough" diamond does not look like anything special.

All diamonds are very old; they were formed at least 1 billion years ago. They were made deep inside the Earth, under crushing pressure and great heat.

^This rare blue diamond gets its color from a tiny amount of the element boron.

Silicon gems

Emeralds, topaz, garnets, and amethysts are some of the many gems that contain silicon.

⌄ **An emerald gets its green color from the elements chromium and vanadium.**

⌄ **Minerals that grow in a hole in a rock, like this amethyst, are called geodes.**

^ **Garnets are often found in igneous and metamorphic rocks.**

Silicon is a very hard element. When it joins together with elements that give it color, it can make gorgeous gems.

Ruby and sapphire

Rubies and sapphires are different colors of the mineral corundum. They are some of the most expensive gems of all.

⌄ A large ruby can cost more than a diamond. It gets its red color from chromium.

« Sapphire is made blue by the mineral ilmenite.

Corundum is made of aluminum and oxygen. It is the second hardest mineral, after diamond. Pure corundum is brown, but other elements give it lovely colors.

> ⌃ A star sapphire is a sapphire that contains a crystal of the mineral rutile.

Glossary

amber Tree resin that has hardened over millions of years. Resin is a substance that oozes from some trees and plants.

carbonate A mineral that has the elements carbon and oxygen as its main ingredients.

crust The outer layer of Earth, made of igneous, metamorphic, and sedimentary rocks.

crystal A symmetrical shape formed by a mineral. It is created by the elements linking up in a pattern.

element A simple, most basic substance. There are 115 elements, including oxygen, silicon, carbon, and gold.

evaporate To change from a runny liquid into a gas.

fertilizer A material that provides nutrients that help plants grow.

fossil The hardened remains of an animal or plant that lived many millions of years ago.

fuel A material that is burned to make heat or power.

gas A substance that is not solid or runny. Air is made of gases.

gem A mineral valued for its strength, clearness, or its color.

hot spring A place where water flows to the surface after being heated inside Earth.

igneous A type of rock that is made when hot, runny magma cools down and hardens.

magma Hot, melted rock that lies beneath Earth's surface.

metamorphic A type of rock that is made when any rock is changed by enormous heat and pressure.

mineral A solid that is formed by nature, inside the Earth or in water. Each mineral is a mix of particular elements. If a mineral has room to grow, it will form a crystal.

pressure The force created when something presses or pushes against something else.

quarry A place where rock is dug from the ground.

rock A solid substance that is made of minerals.

rust When a reddish, powdery coating forms on iron. It is caused by water or damp air.

seam A mineral layer sandwiched between other rocks.

sedimentary Rock formed when pebbles, mud, minerals, or plant and animal remains are pressed together until they harden.

solid Firm and with a fixed shape. A solid is not runny or a gas.

Index

A

amber 14, 60
amethyst 56
apatite 50
aragonite 7, 46, 47
azurite 41

B

basalt 18–19

C

calcite 31, 46, 47, 50
chalk 4, 32–33
cinnabar 51
clay 27, 28, 29, 30, 34–35
coal 36–37
conglomerate 30
corundum 58, 59

DE

diamond 54–55, 58, 59
emerald 56
epidote 40

F

feldspar 6, 19, 51
flint 32
fluorite 48

G

garnet 56, 57
gneiss 25
gold 42, 43, 50
grandidierite 53
granite 6, 17
graphite 49

HJ

hornfels 25
jadeite 45

LM

lazurite 44

limestone 4, 26, 27, 38–39, 47

marble 26–27

O

obsidian 20–21

oolite 31

opal 52

P

pegmatite 16

pumice 22–23

pyrite 41

QR

quartz 6, 32, 45, 49

quartzite 11

rhyolite 17

ruby 58

S

salt 49

sandstone 10, 11, 31

sapphire 58–59

schist 24

serpentine 9

shale 28

silicon 6, 7, 41; 44, 45, 56, 57

slate 28–29

T

tourmaline 53

topaz 56

Picture Credits

(t=top, b=bottom, l=left, r=right, c=centre)

Front cover Andrewsound95/Dreamstime **Back cover** tl Rinus Baak/Dreamstime, tc Leventina/Dreamstime, tr Vulkanette/Dreamstime, c Susan Caroll/Dreamstime, bl Ken Backer/Dreamstime, br Grassetto/iStock.

Dreamstime
6 bl Malewitch, 7 cr Jiri Vaclavek, 10–11 b Satori13, 16 cr Iluzia, 17 tl Michal Baranski. 18 tl Kushnirov Avraham, 21 tr Speshilov Sergey , 22 bl Ulianna19970, 22–23 Ajafoto, 24–25 Jukka Palm, 25 br Les Palenik, 28–29 Nooscapes, 36–37 Dmytro Tolmachov, 39 tr Honourableandbold, 41 tr Carlosvelayos, 42–43 Roman Bodnarchuk, 45 br Sergey Lavrentev, 46–47 Goldnelk, 48 bl Epitavi, 50–51 Wieslaw Jarek, 50 br Juice Images, 51 tr Danolsen, 53 tr Jasmin Awad, 54–55 Richard Thomas, 56–57 Saraizzo, 56 bl Simon Zenger, 58 bl Mrreporter, 64 br Mrreporter.

Getty Images
4–5 b Stockbyte.

iStock.com
1 bc Gilles_Paire, 2–3 b koi88, 4 bl Maui01, 4 c hsvrs, 6–7 b jopelka, 8 bl bluerabbit, 8–9 b GISBA, 9 bl Zanozaru, 10 bl George Clerk, 11 cr dmitriyd, 12–13 b Ivan Nakonechnyy, 13 tr the-lightwriter, 16–17 b Rich Legg, 18–19 b pabradyphoto, 20–21 b jatrax, 26–27 sabirmallick, 27 tl Baloncici, 28 bl northlightimages, 29 cr Peter Hermus, 30 bl mikeuk, 32–33 Auke Holwerda, 34–35 DenisTangneyJr, 34 bl PavelZahorec, 35 br Holger Mette, 37 cb Andrew Cribb, 37 tr indykb, 38–39 luxiangjian4711, 39 bl Phototreat, 40–41 koi88, 43 cr Gilles_Paire, 44–45 mj0007, 44 bl J-Palys, 46 cl MarcelC, 47 br hsvrs, 48–49 PhongTranVN, 52–53 Vadim Svirin, 52 bl aleskramer, 54 bl Thomas Demarczyk, 57 cr VvoeVale, 62 cr aleskramer, 63 br Gilles_Paire.

Other
12 bl Sandstein, 14–15 Brocken Inaglory, 15 br Ballista, 23 br Robert DuHamel, 30–31 b John Fowler, 31 tr Eurico Zimbres, 32 cl Andreas Trepte, 33 tr James St. John, 36–37 Dmytro Tolmachov, 40 cb Didier Descouens, 42 cl Heinrich Pniok, 58–59 Parent Géry, 61 br Didier Descouens.

Public Domain
19 br NOAA, 25 tl Fed, 55 br Smithsonian Institution Archives.